RESONANCE

~~~~

MANIFESTING YOUR HEART'S DESIRE

Copyright © 2011 by Mark Allen Frost
Published by Seth Returns Publishing
Lake County California
Editorial: Mark Allen Frost
Cover Art, Design, Typography & Layout: Mark Frost

All rights reserved. No part of this book may be reproduced in any form or by any electronic or mechanical means, including photocopying, recording, or information storage and retrieval systems, without permission in writing from the publisher, except by a reviewer, who may quote brief passages in a review.

Library of Congress Control Number: 2011914941
ISBN: 978-0-9826946-5-7

This book is dedicated to all of Seth's clients who have received his guidance in phone sessions and at our events. Thanks for your support. Special thanks to Carol Joy and Richard Strauss for proof reading and typographical assistance.

CONTENTS

Introduction by Mark...........................vii
Preface...xi

LEXICON OF THE VISIONARY.................................1
ESSENTIAL METAPHORS..11
THE PRACTICE..21
RESONANCE DYNAMICS..43
THE REGIMENS..59
PROBABLE OUTCOMES...81
Q AND A WITH SETH..89

Epilogue................................105
Ritual of Sanctuary.................107
Glossary.................................109
Ordering Page........................115

Note: Please do not take any of the information given in this book as medical advice. Follow the directions of your medical professional.

Introduction by Mark

Welcome to Seth's new book. This project began some time ago when I was asked by a workshop participant what Seth thought about the Law of Attraction. I had to admit that I did not know, but I said I would ask him. This started a conversation between Seth and myself about what he calls the Ancient Wisdom, and how this information is conveyed to humanity. So this is a book on the Ancient Wisdom, primarily.

Seth also wanted to include the Techniques and Strategies that he uses in his work with clients. This is material that he has developed over the years in phone sessions and at Seth events held in public. He wanted to present the tools that work the best for the people he helps, according to the feedback we get from clients. So this is also a self-help book.

This is a book on theory. His theory that Resonance is at the heart of Reality Creation seems pretty obvious to me now. When we first started putting the book together I looked up some definitions of Resonance and found that Light was mentioned more often than not. Light is short wavelength electromagnetic radiation produced by resonance on an atomic scale, such as electrons in atoms. I can visualize Seth's theorized Consciousness Units active in this definition. Though it seems to me that the activity of his CUs takes place quite a bit beyond the atomic.

And this is a book on the Seth Teaching. I'm a student just like Seth's other students. Seth is the teacher and he is coming from a particular point of view. The magical perspective, he calls it. It is empowered, it is difficult to master, it is very effective once you do the work and create a habit out of the Techniques. The magic is not in the Techniques or the words themselves but in how you internalize the material. I think this point is key.

Rather than thinking in terms of what you SHOULD believe - according to Seth, this creates resistance, static, dissonance - just try out all of the Techniques and select the ones that work for you, those that Resonate with you and for you. Then you can form your Practice from what works, just as I am doing with what works for me.

I see it as a practice of Loving the reality into being, consciously, as a co-creator. It is a challenge for me to tune into this Loving Understanding that Seth talks

Introduction by Mark

about. As I said, I have Lessons to learn. I have Issues just like everyone else.

I am impressed by the way Seth can create a Trance State in the reader through his narrative. Contrary to what some might think, it seems to me that the effect is more profound if you know that he does this and you can anticipate it. Then you can acknowledge it to yourself as not just a phantom of consciousness but a real phenomenon.

And I Love the way Seth uses humor and wordplay to put the reader at ease. His definition of Dialogue is a case in point. Dialogue, to talk through, as in discussing a subject. Or Dialogue, to talk through, as in having a channeled source speak through you. It is a pun. It has double meanings and works on different levels of consciousness, as puns do. When you engage in the Seth Teaching, you are inviting your Higher Centers of Awareness to Dialogue with you. This is what waking up is all about. Just my two cents. Have fun!

Preface

We are now referring to my new material as a Teaching, as a Path of Awakening. It is a path toward independence, generally, away from authority figures and towards a realization that the answers to all questions are to be found within the personal consciousness: your personal consciousness. As a student of your own existence, you are expected to examine your thoughts, beliefs, and behaviors as a scientist would, a Scientist of Consciousness. Because you are studying yourself, objectively, Lovingly, you will observe instances of denial, intellectualization, cynicism, egoic pontifications, and so on. The negative emotions are noted, their origins identified, as plans are implemented to transform these negative states of consciousness into their opposites.

This is the crux of the matter. The student of the Personal Reality attempts to fine-tune the expression of Reality Creation for the highest good of all. Why "the highest good of all?" When you make your Transition do you wish to die alone, or with the entirety of existence - the Universes - supporting you?

Now please observe that I am addressing you as a particular type of human. Obviously there may be readers of this manuscript who are not on-board with us in these arcane studies. These directions are not for this type. And this is where the concept of Resonance comes in quite profoundly. If this material does not Resonate with you on some level, if it does not pique your interest and compel you to read on, it is probably not for you. Resonance, you see. It is at the foundation of all activities in Reality Creation.

Let me remind you that we suggest continuous use of the Ritual of Sanctuary as you perfect your Practice and carry out your Regimens. The Ritual of Sanctuary is explained in the back of this book. Good Luck.

Lexicon of the Visionary

You are in your system to learn how to use energy to create what you want…

The New Age Canon

"I am on Earth to be happy." "It all works out for the best." "There are no accidents." "Everything happens for a reason." "Each cloud has a silver lining." "There is an inner world that gives birth to the outer." "You create your own reality." These are some of your modern sayings from the New Age, metaphysical, and spiritual genres of literature. They each have a sense of magic about them, do they not? The very notion that, "You create your own reality" - my contribution to this New Age canon - holds within it the presumption of power, of fertile creative energy.

Now I have some good news for you. If you subscribe to these magical Precepts you are certainly on the right track in your evolution. For you ARE on Earth to be

> **Seth's Soapbox - Issues & Lessons**
> If you are poor and you wish to be wealthy, you have a Prosperity Issue. Your Lesson, then, might be to use your creative energy to create prosperity for the highest good of all, including you and your family.

happy, Dear Reader. This is quite true. And you do create your own reality, what we now call the Personal Reality Field in my books. Specifically, you are in your system to learn how to use energy to create what you want, what you desire.

I am Seth and I speak to you from a particular perspective, one that is outside of your much theorized space/time continuum. I see that some of you may doubt this statement. Some of you fear that you are in your dimension to suffer and experience pain and disappointment - at least for the better part of the journey - on the way to another highly theorized locale you call "heaven." This limited perception is a gift from your ancestors and others who have taught you through religious conditioning the "benefits" and perhaps "spirituality" of Lack.

You could say that these New Age concepts answer the question, "Why am I on Earth?" in a very affirmative fashion. This movement, indeed, is a response to the naysayers, those who have controlled you for many hundreds of years. The New Agers emphasize the Virtues of Humanity, the experiencing of Love and pleasure by everyone, healthy self-esteem with an absence of shame, guilt, and the other detrimental states of consciousness. I think that you can immediately sense how this perspective - we shall call it the Visionary Perspective - challenges the status quo espoused by your governments, your mainstream religions, your military establishments, your Negative Media, and other authorities.

Waking Up

Another important aspect of this perspective is that of Awakening. We are creating this manuscript for the person who is waking-up to their greater reality. Indeed, this material will not make sense to you if you are otherwise.

How can you tell if you are one of these people?
Take this simple quiz: (Humorously)

- ◆ Do you find that you are deep in your Issues and Lessons, the reasons you came to Earth at this time?
- ◆ Are you attracted to the various spiritual movements of your era?
- ◆ Are you experiencing graphic demonstrations in your Personal Reality of The Shift in consciousness and other so-called "supernatural" phenomena?

◆ Do you sense that time is somehow speeding up for you, as though you are quickly coming to the brink of a great transformation?

> **Seth's Soapbox - Intent**
> Your Free Will choices determine the specifics of how you create your reality. We also call this perspective Intent or Divine Will when it is informed by the Higher Centers of Awareness.

The Visionary Perspective

All of these are indicators that you are experiencing the Visionary Perspective in your lifetime. This perspective has a particular vocabulary associated with it as well as other elements that help to distinguish it from other perspectives. Here in this book we will discuss some of these metaphysical concepts. We will remind you that this information is timeless, for it is always there within your consciousness in all of your lives. And we hope to demonstrate that we are all talking about the same thing, here. The spiritual authors from your present timeframe, the metaphysicians from your past, ALL of us are presenting this material in our own ways, in our own words, for the enlightenment of the average citizen of your world.

Lexicon of the Visionary

Ancient Wisdom

The New Age canon has a source that is as ancient as the Earth herself. We call this source the Ancient Wisdom. In great cycles of expression, at appropriate times in your history, this information rises up within the collective consciousness and <u>insists</u> on acknowledgement. Naturally it is the expressive among you who first heed this call. You are prompted by these impulses to express yourself, to express your vision. It is no coincidence, therefore, when the visionary content shows similarities across vastly different populations from all over your Earth.

Look around you at your modern media. In every country of the world you will find the visionary artists creating their works for the highest good of all. The essence of these works is the same regardless of the tongue or the territory. From the collective consciousness of All That Is, the ancient truths are finding a voice, right when this material is needed the most.

Visionary Experience

Now this communication stream presents to succeeding generations a context for awakening to the inner world. But it is not obvious, at least at first. It is there in <u>potential</u> to be drawn-in to the personal consciousness. This occurs during the practices of your spiritual traditions, and also in your accidental visitations to the Unknown Reality. Here are some examples: When you are taken out of your body in nature as you witness the majesty of a natural event, such as a thunder storm; or when you experience a deeply moving encounter with the animal kingdom; or when you encounter a "ghost" or other non-physical being; or when you experience extreme negative emotion or even pleasure. Though you may not be looking for it, you are finding Spirit, and you are <u>thoroughly</u> transformed during these Moments of Awakening.

What can you do when you are faced with the numinous? My answer is this: "Change your behaviors, enlarge your beliefs, use your Intent to embrace the transformation you are witnessing. Embody it, my friend." If you do, you will be altered to the core, 'to the nth degree,' as we also say.

Trajectories - Perspectives - Processes

The following descriptions of consciousness activity in the Third Dimension are framed in terms of polarity, trajectories of evolution, states of consciousness, and so on. Here we hope to portray the vast field of possible visionary experience in a concise form. These are terms we use with our clients to describe phenomena such as: remembering the Ancient Wisdom, the Awakening, and the Healing Journey.

> **Seth's Soapbox - Telepathy**
> In the Telepathic Network that supports all activities in the Third Dimension, you are connected to everything via the Consciousness Units. This connectivity enables the emergence into your world of your day-to-day realities with some consistency.

Exercise: Where Are You Now?

Just for fun, please jot down where you would place yourself on some of these trajectories of development. This will give us a benchmark that we will use to chart your progress as you diligently complete the exercises in this manuscript. (Humorously)

For example, referring to our chart:
Are you on a Healing Voyage in your existence? Or are you lurching forward in the Common Trance, oblivious to your surroundings, focused only on your subconscious desire to belong to the group?
Are you somewhere in between with the vast majority of humans?
Take a few moments to work with this material...

Resonance - Manifesting Your Heart's Desire

Trajectories - Perspectives - Processes

Unlucky - Lucky
Fear of Pleasure - Ecstasy
The Mundane - The Exalted
Status Quo - Visionary
Job - Quest
Rat Race - Healing Journey
The Paycheck - The Abundant Universe
Common Trance - Uncommon Trance
Obey Authority - Self-Authority
Sleeping - Awakening
Subconscious Creation - Conscious Co-creation
Holding On - Letting Go
Assessing - Going With The Flow
Tension - Release
Past - Future
Persona - Guides
ego/intellect - Higher Gestalts
Awakened Self
Soul Self
Objective Observer
Reincarnational
Personal Reality - Consensus Reality
magician shaman witch

Lexicon of the Visionary

Sick - Wounded Healer
Precept - Percept
Consumerism - Healing Journey
Negative Creation - Positive Reality
Status Quo - The New World
Worst Case - Best Case
Denial - Personal Responsibility
Intellectualization - Visionary Perspective
Trance State

NOTES

Through the Hidden World

Now I hope I have not lost you with these discussions of ancient Precepts, telepathy, and the etheric world. I am laying the groundwork for our exploration of manifestation through Resonance and this will be a passage through the hidden world. It is the steady path I take when presenting this information to you in my manuscripts.

Feel free to consult the Glossary at the back of the book if you are having trouble following my narrative. And please keep an open mind and do discount, at least for the time being, the admonitions of the ego/intellect to put this book down and run away. (Humorously) And now, on with the show...

ESSENTIAL METAPHORS

You are fine-tuning these ancient affirmative statements to suit your own needs and desires…

The Promise of Magic

This current manuscript is quite similar, a cousin you might say, to the work I created with Jane Roberts and her husband: ***The Magical Way***. This IS the magical way I am offering to you, updated of course, to be agreeable to the modern sensibility. Notice how these empowering statements of mine offer to you-the-reader the promise of magic, of Soulful creativity, of manifestation of the heart's desire.

Many of the statements I use in this book are Essential Metaphors; metaphors for the activity of consciousness in your dimension. They <u>are</u> essential, in the sense that they are necessary to this Teaching of mine; they are required so that the student can comprehend the system. They are also essential in that they contain the <u>essence</u>

of what they purport to represent. Let me go on a bit concerning this very important idea.

Thinking back to my Soapbox description of The Telepathic Network... This Essential Metaphor suggests a subtext or an intuition that you ARE in a reciprocal relationship with everything in your world. It is an idea that <u>wants</u> you to comprehend it. Do you grasp the meaning here? These essences are POTENTIALLY active. They are activated by your Intent, or what you may also call your Will. Please keep this in mind as you make your way through this manuscript.

> **Seth's Soapbox - Subtext**
> The unspoken truth of a statement that is sensed intuitively. It can come in a burst of intuition or quite subtly, as in a growing understanding.

Resonance is a Metaphor

Now that I have presented some introductory material, we will now discuss the Essential Metaphor that is the subject of this book. Resonance: a very high concept indeed. It is a broad, over-reaching Essential Metaphor that may help you discover those aspects of your consciousness that can help you to create what you wish to create.

Essential Metaphors

In our book on the Soul Family, we first defined Resonance in this way, *"What is created intentionally and with power on the inner world is manifest in the outer world through Resonance - the electromagnetic assemblage of Consciousness Units into Reality Constructs."* This is Resonance with a capital R, you see. This is the activity that creates positive realities for the Practitioner.

Let me now add to this definition by expanding on the word "thoughtful." By thoughtful what I mean is… BOTH subconscious and what you might call "intentionally" conscious thought create the reality that you then observe as feedback. The awakening student becomes aware of the particulars within the subconscious mind.

This accounts for the phenomenon of the Moment of Awakening in which the student realizes that they do indeed create their less-than-positive realities, and that they do so <u>subconsciously</u>, for the most part, through negative ruminations. This we may call resonance with a small "r," if you don't mind. These negative ruminations create negative realities. They are the opposites of the positive thought forms - the Precepts, for example - we suggest you use to create your <u>positive</u> realities. I am speaking of the positive circular thoughts that you create and then Ritually inculcate into your mental awareness.

> **Seth's Soapbox - Ruminations**
> Negative realities are given life through repetitive negative thoughts, images, and emotions. Positive realities are created by repetitive positive thoughts, images, and emotions.

Resonance in Action

The oscillating emotional tone, the Feeling-Tone that also has thought and imagery attached to it, is this Resonance we are describing to you. Resonance is the frequency of creation in your world. It oscillates multi-dimensionally, also, to create perceived realities within all of your Simultaneous Existences. The specific frequency of oscillation or vibration is determined by the varying inputs of emotion, thought, and imagery. In each of your lives you exhibit the specific frequency of that life. No two are exactly the same.

Personalized

Now, as you begin to "try on" some of these empowered concepts - including Resonance - it becomes necessary for you to personalize them to your particular Issue that you have discovered, the Lesson that you are learning, or the manifestation project you are initiating. By making it personal, you are fine-tuning these affirmative statements to suit your own needs and desires. Thus, it will be the Essential Metaphors that you-the-reader define for yourself that will have the most power and integrity in your creative endeavors. I will guide you through this process so that you may maintain the power of the Precept, while still configuring and adapting it to reflect your goals.

For example, You create your own reality may become, "I (Your Name) AM the captain of my ship!" "I have the power of the magician in my world," or more specifically, "I have the limitless power of All That Is within me to create my prosperous life for myself and my family." Then you might go about your waking reality using our Techniques, proving this to yourself through your behaviors, through your thoughts, through your feelings.

Seth's Soapbox - Embody

The Intentional creator of realities embodies the Essential Metaphors. By embody, I mean, you walk, you talk, you feel, you <u>believe</u> the concept into actuality.

Useful Metaphors

These concepts were first presented in our book ***Thought Reality***. They represent some of my interpretations of the Ancient Wisdom material. Once activated, they have the potential to assist you in the creation of what you **Love**. You may think of these statements as the foundational elements of your Practice and of the Regimens to follow.

Exercise: Sensing the Precepts

For now, please read these Precepts and ask yourself which of them may be of the most help in your life. This is a beginning exercise in Resonance Dynamics. You simply achieve a light Trance, a relaxed inner-directed mental state. You are looking for a subdued state of consciousness that allows you to read this material and internalize it - be affected by it - without falling asleep. Stretch your body, close your eyes, relax into a comfortable position. Do what you do when you meditate, Dear Reader. Now read on...

You create your own reality.

Please do take me literally. For you ARE the literal fabricator of your existence. With the energy of the cosmos - of All That Is - you co-create all that you see before you, as well as all that you indeed ARE in this moment, including your physical body. Does this remind you of something?

Essential Metaphors

You are connected to everything in your world.
In this collaborative moment, within your Personal Reality Field, you are supported by, and you do indeed support EVERYTHING around you. These energetic supports are observable to the nth degree. In other words, you could follow with your Inner Senses the strands of connective energy between you and everything in your world and find a part of you in everything else.

You can change the Consensus Reality from your Personal Reality Field.
Your individual consciousness energy goes out from your Personal Reality Field into the Consensus Reality Field to influence the manifestation of collective realities. In a sense, you could say that you vote within the collective with your thoughts, your images, and your emotions. They have effects on the global manifestation.

Emotion is the creative energy of All That Is in action.
Your thoughts and images are actualized according to the frequency of the emotion you give to them. Please note the suggestion of the Resonance activity in this definition.

Human consciousness is founded in Love.
Your primal condition at all times and in all lives is Love. We affirm the keynote of your world religions and

most spiritual practices. Again, we are speaking literally, here.

Diversions from Love through Negative Emotions create Negative Realities.
By habitually diverting your attention to Negative Emotion from Love you begin to habitually create Lack, illness, and other Negative Realities.

All imbalances may be corrected through Love and Courage.
With Loving Understanding and Courage you can transform Negative Realities into Positive Realities. This is the primary practice of this Teaching of mine.

You are the sum of your Simultaneous Lives within your current Moment Point.
Your Essential Identity in this moment is created from the consciousness material within the mental environments of all of your Simultaneous Lives. Within the identified Moment Point, you have access to any and all of these Reincarnational Existences. Try it.

Your Inner Senses may be used to examine and change anything past, present or future.
In the Trance state, within your current Moment Point, you can transform events from your past, present or future.

Essential Metaphors

You are in telepathic rapport with everything in your world.

The Consciousness Units (See Glossary) of which you are composed Resonate with the CUs of which everything else is made.

Reality Constructs are composed of Consciousness Units of awarized energy.

Everything in your system is created out of CUs of awareized energy that are telepathic and holographic.

Coordinate Points permeate matter and space and modulate the activity of the Consciousness Units.

Coordinate Points in space and time hold the form of Reality Constructs created by consciousness.

Your Intention, Emotions and Beliefs provide the energy and direction for Reality Creation.

By changing your focus, your emotions, and your beliefs, you change your reality. You will realize this as you complete the exercises in this book.

Everything exists initially as Gestalts of Consciousness, the nonphysical "templates" of creation.

Thoughts, images, and emotions assemble in arrays of potentiality in the pre-manifestation domain. These assemblages act as the blueprints for Reality Constructs of all types.

I realize that I am being somewhat repetitive in these Precepts, "redundant," as you say. I do this because repetition is the key to teaching, and it is the key to learning also.

Can you sense how some of these statements lend themselves quite naturally to certain projects rather than others? Can you also sense the phenomenon we identify as Resonance active in these Precepts?

Exercise: Personalize Your Favorite Precepts

This is a writing exercise, primarily. Without thinking about it too much, choose those few Precepts that speak to you, that you feel may be true or useful to you. Then personalize each of them by placing yourself at the center of the idea. You will be putting your personal energy into the Precepts as you do this, just in working with the material. You will have the opportunity of using this material later in this manuscript.

The Practice

If you are the captain of your ship act as though you are the captain of your ship...

The Quest

Why are you reading this book? As I stated earlier, I make an assumption that you are looking for something that is lacking in your life. So I am assuming that you are on a Quest of some sort. Perhaps you are on a Healing Voyage to correct a malady, or you are experiencing Lack in a quite profound way and wish to discover the Abundant Universe for yourself, or you may be lonely, looking for your ideal partner - the Soul Mate - and wondering how to go about that. Are you a student of your own life, one who investigates the Personal Reality as a philosopher? Do you notice the mystical intrusions from the Unknown Reality, the anomalies of consciousness, and attempt to uncover their source?

Resonance - Manifesting Your Heart's Desire

These descriptions assume you are looking for your own answers to important questions in your life, as though you were on a Journey, a Quest. Do you see how these Essential Metaphors denoting progress, learning, and adventure give a fullness of meaning to your activities in the Third Dimension?

This how it works, Dear Reader…
Referring to our chart in Chapter One: When you identify yourself as being on a Path of Awakening you <u>catalyze</u> the energies of awakening within you. When you Embody the Essential Metaphor called the Path of Awakening, you gradually see your world change to reflect this new perspective. Everything becomes a Lesson when you see your life in this way. Your Issues are revealed to you in the intimacy of daily living. You are indeed awakening to your greater reality as you Resonate your new world into being

> **Seth's Soapbox - Percept/Precept**
> Perception (Percept) creates reality in the Third Dimension. Thus, when you habitually embody the Essential Metaphors (Precepts) your perceived world begins to change to reflect the essences of these Precepts. Prove it to yourself.

The Practice

Loving Understanding and Courage

Now the Path of Awakening we offer here is initially concerned with two very powerful perspectives: Loving Understanding and Courage. It is quite simple…

As you live your life, you go about your day confronting your Issues head-on, without denial and without intellectualization. If an associate tells you something negative about yourself, for example, you consider it, you muse upon it and wonder if this might be an Issue. Courageously you move forward with this information, asking the Universe, in a sense, "Is this true? Does this apply to me?" If the negative material is true, you begin learning your Lesson by taking responsibility for this Issue and the harm you have caused to yourself and others, perhaps. You are understanding your Issue in a Loving way, with humility, you see. So it is also quite profound, here, and let me tell you why...

Because you create your own reality. When you Embody these Precepts, when you learn your Lessons, it sets you up for creating Loving and Courageous realities. This becomes Intentional Reality Creation. You are transformed on this simple path.

Referring to the previous example… If you have taken to heart the criticism of your associate and you are working on yourself to clear this up, you will, after a length of time, experience the amelioration of the negative trait. You may then expect the associate to comment on it, having noticed the change.

Time and the Percept

The physics of this for those of you who would care to know, referring to my previous soapbox... The Percept creates the Reality Construct from Consciousness Units AND THEN perceives it. Do not be confused by time in this discussion, therefore. The Percept uses time as a structure for creative activity. In truth, outside of time in the Unknown Reality, everything happens at once. Thus, the Percept organizes, allots, schedules the creative efforts of consciousness, forming things and events from chaos.

The Divine is Imperative

Additionally, I do believe that your connection to a Higher Awareness is imperative in these explorations. For in terms of states of consciousness - the various perspectives that the Practitioner Embodies in this method - would it not be of value to seek out the elevated perspectives of the nonphysical beings, the Energy Personality, the Guides, the gods and goddesses, your own Higher Consciousness?

The Practice

It makes sense, I think, to receive what you might call, a "second opinion," here, moving forward with your studies. Yes, you are certain of what you the ego/intellect know and what you wish to find out. However, when you invoke the Higher Gestalts of Consciousness "the entire game plan changes," to coin a phrase. All of your behaviors, all of your thoughts and emotions become understood in an entirely different way when you make these connections. It is indeed an altered state, a highly elevated and exalted state of consciousness when the student is connected to the Source.

Your Responsibility

Yes, only God can make a tree. I totally concur. However, in this Teaching of mine we are asking you-the-reader to acknowledge your divinity. You are God and Goddess and you are All That Is. Observe through your particular perspective, therefore, your creations in the collaborative effort with your environment. Now when I ask you to look at what you are doing, see where you are going, take responsibility for your Reality Creation, this is what I mean. With the full appreciation of "what you are doing," you are compelled by conscience to take responsibility and CHANGE YOUR CREATIONS FOR THE BETTER.

Techniques and Strategies

Our phone clients and our students who read our books have found these Techniques and Strategies to be the most beneficial. Please remember to conduct regularly the Ritual of Sanctuary described at the back of the book.

The Trance State
This is, of course, the state of consciousness marked by relaxation, an inward focus, and what you might call a "tuneable" connection to the Unknown Reality. How you enter this state is up to you. Through practicing entering and exiting this state, you learn how to lessen or deepen at-will this Trance. I believe I will leave it at that, on the assumption that you are well-versed in achieving these states of sacred awareness. You ARE awakening at this time…

Exercise: Belief Assessment
It is not a matter of seeing and then believing, it is a case of believing AND THEN seeing. Your Personal Reality Field is a DIRECT reflection of your beliefs about what you think is possible. The task, then, is to determine what are your beliefs. Then you might attempt to condition these beliefs of yours so that they are enlarged, en-

ergized, modified to suit your awakening consciousness. In other words, you would want to change your beliefs to allow for a perception of your heart's desire. This is entirely achievable, Dear Reader.

Your beliefs are accessible to you in the form of Feeling-Tones. (See Glossary) So rather than try to describe in detail what you believe your beliefs ARE, simply relax for a few moments and describe to yourself, in written or in another form, how you <u>feel</u> about the primary domains of existence. These domains might include relationships, prosperity, health, the spiritual, your sexuality.

As you express yourself honestly with regards to these aspects of your life, you may find that feelings arise for you to be noticed. You may then sense that there is imagery attached to the feelings as events from the past come to mind. There may also be other sensory information connected to this Feeling-Tone. Now as a sum of feeling, emotion, and other sensory material, you have this assessment of your beliefs. Document it in the medium of your choice.

Polarizing the Negative Material

With this assessment of your beliefs I suggest you begin to experiment. In this exercise, you may polarize the negative Feeling-Tones that you have discovered in your belief analysis. By polarize, I mean you may create in your consciousness the OPPOSITE of the negative emotion, thought, and imagery you have discovered. In a sense, you are finding something good, something of possible value in even the negative material of consciousness. Let me go on...

Now, not only does every cloud have a silver lining, as the saying goes, but in my view, literally EVERYTHING in created reality has this positive potential. Your focus on this positive potential CREATES it, you see. This is a re-statement of our Consecutive Positive Assessment Technique from previous books.

The Premanifestation Domain

Observing the natural Resonance phenomenon...

Suppose you are using your Intent to "keep a good thought," for you are challenged by negative thoughts and imagery that you have found in your belief assessment. As these positive thoughts are expressed within your consciousness, perhaps they also reflect positive imagery, positive emotion, and so on. This material literally <u>seeks</u> out within your personal consciousness and within the collective consciousness, validation. It tries to express itself. Do you see?

Now these expressions align in what we call the pre-manifestation domain. This is a sort of "holding area" for

Reality Constructs <u>before</u> they "bloom" into your world. In arrays of potentiality, then, these etheric Gestalts of Consciousness are formed. As you continue your regimen of "keeping a good thought" - turning poison into medicine, another of our Essential Metaphors - your efforts strive to replicate themselves in the physical world. In time, improved Reality Constructs do emerge from the pre-manifestation domain into your Personal Reality Field. They Resonate into being through this process.

The Box

Another Technique that has helped our clients is The Box. This is an exercise from our book on Nine Eleven. Simply visualize a Box suspended around your neck. Now take all of the negative material you have discovered in your belief assessment and put it in The Box. The material is automatically transformed into its opposite. What does not support your heart's desire, you see, is transformed into supportive energies for the <u>creation</u> of your heart's desire. When you open up The Box at a later time, you may be pleasantly surprised to see what you have created. No energy is lost, here, it simply takes another form.

Issues and Lessons come into play, also. As you change your beliefs, as you face your Issues and learn your Lessons, energy is released for creative purposes.

The energy you once used to deny and intellectualize and repress Issues and avoid your Lessons becomes available for growth: spiritual growth.

Good Humor and the Magical Child

My ongoing students are well aware of my theory of Good Humor and its place in the creation of positive realities. Briefly, the Practitioner may use simple humor and a self-created sense of good will that may lead to the creation of improved realities.

One way to begin this is to assume the identity of the Magical Child. This is the Essential Identity of you-the-reader, the child BEFORE you were frustrated, before you were spun off on a negative trajectory of development, perhaps, before you became socialized.

Playful innocence also describes this benign state of awareness. Your countenance glows with good will, here. You have a smile on your face and you are quite pleased with yourself and your world. Because you have not yet forgotten that you are a wonder-worker, you still know how to create what you want, what you desire. You even have within your mental environment memories of preceding lives. You have not been forced to forget this material. Am I getting through to you, Dear Reader? This is the foundational state of your consciousness. This is Love. Begin here to create your positive realities.

Putting into Practice

Your Practice as an awakening human, one who is intentionally creating positive realities, entails putting into practice the Essential Metaphors. Again, for example: "I am the captain of my ship." Are you? If you are the captain of your ship act as though you are the captain of your ship. Walk like a captain, talk like a captain, immerse yourself in the role of the captain. Create your reality with purposeful Intent. Do you see my meaning here?

I do not wish to be too hard on you in this manuscript. However, if you wish to dramatically change your reality for the better, you must surely do something dramatically different in your existence. And even though I am being somewhat humorous in this example, please observe the subtext, here.

Pretending or Manifesting

Though this Practice is related to pretending, there is a great difference between conscious manifesting and pretending. Let me describe these differences briefly...

In conscious manifesting, at least in my view, the Highest Perspective is invoked throughout the Practice, throughout your Rituals, Regimens and studies. I submit that pretending does not require a connection to these Evolved Perspectives.

In pretending, there is also the playful approach that I see as a requirement in the Practice. However, this playful approach must be grounded, in my opinion, in the Higher Centers. The Divine Child or the Magical Child is invoked, as I have just said. This may most easily occur when you have an ongoing connection to your Guides, to your Energy Personality, to All That Is.

Additionally, in the act of pretending there is lacking a complete faithful expectation in the successful outcome, as I see it. You are not manifesting with Divine Intent the desired Reality Constructs or events. Pretending is a good start, in other words, however, please invoke the powerful non-physical beings if you are committed to conscious manifesting.

I do believe that some of my readers are neglecting the differences. The key here, is FIRST to connect with your Source, your Guidance, your Higher Consciousness. Then the Ancient Wisdom is revealed. Then you are indeed Guided to your destination. Then you are not alone; you have the resources of the Divine at your disposal.

Bridges of Consciousness

In a related matter, (Humorously) I am quite able to act as a go-between <u>between</u> you, Dear Reader, and your Energy Personality and other Guides. This I offer as a service to my readers, to help you get connected.

The Practice

Therefore, use my Techniques, use this material, use my felt-presence as a bridge between your Earthly perceptions and your Guidance. You simply ask for the connections to be made in self-reflective states and when you are in nature. Then you would anticipate a positive result. Because you are connecting with the Seth entity through your Practice, you will receive this support.

> **Seth's Soapbox - Resonance Factors**
> Creative elements within consciousness that precognate the manifestation. Memories of your future, in a sense, from your greater progressed self.

Metaphorical Tools

These additions to your Practice are also Essential Metaphors. They are visualized devices and important tools you may use to explore and work within the Unknown Reality. For example, you may use your creativity to create, in the Trance State, various modes of transportation to use in your experiments in consciousness. Or you may summon up a diagnostic tool of your own device, that you may use to test, to validate, to sharpen the manifestation.

As with the Trance State, I am assuming you are already a user of the Metaphorical Tools. You may not refer to them as such, but it does seem that most explorers have a strategy, a Technique, a way of going about preparing for and indeed, entering and studying the individual and collective consciousness.

Three Assessments
&
Filling In the Blanks

Now this Ritual Practice I offer you is perfected over time, through practice, practice, practice… With mastery of these Techniques the student begins to awaken more fully. The Three Assessments, Filling in the Blanks, the Resonance Dynamics and the Regimens in the following chapters are offered for your assistance in taking the next step by applying these principles in a very personal way. These may be considered self-improvement projects with an important difference: your reliance on the Ancient Wisdom technologies.

1 - Assessing Your Current Feeling-Tone

This is the first step in a four step process. In this Technique, you consider the Feeling-Tone that reflects your current state of Reality Creation. Remember that the Feeling-Tone has thought, imagery, emotion, and other sensory inputs. It is the energetic signature of a state of consciousness, an event, or even a lifetime. Here we are assessing your current Reality Creation to set a benchmark to compare against future improved realities. How do you feel now?

This is a perspective you might call Honest Assessment, Objective Discernment, or any other descriptive term that connotes prejudice-free sensing of the Personal Reality. You do this from an Observer's Perspective that we have described in the Glossary. You project your consciousness into this aspect which sees you-the-reader in your totality, in your environment, within your niche, as it were, of Third-Dimensional Reality. The information you receive in this assessment is expressed in your favorite medium.

You simply relax, again, as you have done in previous exercises, and go within briefly. The idea is to ask yourself for this information to be made available to your conscious mind. The sensory data that does come up is remembered upon coming out of Trance and is documented for analysis later. This is the Status Quo Reality Feeling-Tone.

2 - Assessing the Best Case Scenario

In its most basic form, this entails delineating in detail your Ideal Objective, what we term the Best Case Scenario "BCS." This is done though writing down the specifics of what you want to create, without consideration, for now, of what you are currently creating. Your imagination is allowed full reign over your expressive powers. If you wish to paint or draw a picture to express this BCS, do so. If you are a dancer and you wish to create a spontaneous dance to express this, do so. Express your Ideal Objective in whatever medium you wish.

To manifest the heart's desire or any improvement, you may first consider what a successful creation looks like, sounds like, feels like, and so on.

Again, in the Trance state you visit a probable future in which you are experiencing this Best Case Scenario. This would be the visualized result of your manifestation activities. Some might call this image the perfected state. Others would assess it as merely moderately improved. You are the one who determines the specifics of this Best Case Scenario. Just as you have done before, you come up to surface awareness from your Trance State and document this idealized vision.

3 - Assessing the Felt Difference

The third step in this analysis concerns going into the meditative state with this information you have gathered from the Status Quo Assessment and from the Best Case Scenario Assessment. You then ask yourself, "What is the difference here between these two states? What is missing in my current reality that is evident in the BCS?" This Feeling-Tone of the Felt Difference will have multi-sensory effects within your consciousness, just as in the other two assessments. You will remember this Felt Difference when you come out of the Trance. You then document this as best you can.

4 - Filling In the Blanks

This is another of our clever metaphors, one that has Good Humor attached to it. It is, in a manner of speaking, "at the other end" of the BCS. This step is one of getting together your Findings from experimentation. These Findings would be the Status Quo, the BCS, and the Felt Difference Assessments. All of the assessments are documented and now is the time to make sure that you are truthful and sure in your documentation. If you find that all is well in these documents, you complete the final step of Filling In the Blanks. This exercise is first done in the waking state, after you examine the Findings. The Felt Difference will contain the elements that are missing from your BCS. In other words, these are the elements that need to be Ritually added to the manifestation to make it more like the BCS. First you do this on paper. Then you do it ritually in the Trance State through Guided Visualization.

This is, briefly what one does in this four step process. Eventually the Practitioner will be adept at this Ritual manifestation to the degree that they would easily do the assessments and Filling in the Blanks exercises throughout the day, whenever it occurred to them to intentionally create their Personal Reality, you see.

Evolving Best Case Scenario "BCS"

The expression of the BCS in physical reality will be governed by how you deal with Issues and Lessons. Thus, you are always approaching the BCS. The relative distance between the mundane and exalted is the creative edge for you, what you use to improve your current Reality Creation.

In this way, as your current reality improves, your consideration of the BCS is altered. You may alter this conception in any way you choose. As Resonance alters your current manifestation, the BCS is changed precisely to that degree. Do you see this important point here? You are the creator. You bring together your world in a collaborative effort with ALL That Is. The Essential Metaphor we are calling Resonance accounts for the energetic transfers of CUs in the moment, from the current Point of Power to the proposed Best Case Scenario Reality. The Best Case Scenario Probable Future is therefore not an end state. It is always mutating, changing frequency and form according to the inputs of CUs from your Essential Identity.

> **Seth's Soapbox - Back Engineering**
> Your faithful expectation that the BCS will manifest CREATES it. You simply visit this probable future and interview yourself as to the particulars of this advanced state of creation.

Back-engineering the BCS

We have also described this process as first Embodying the BCS probable future, and then back-engineering that felt sense, the Feeling-Tone, as best you can. Expectation and positive anticipation charge the whole endeavor. This charge we also call the Empowered Will.

As you continue this practice, you will begin to receive guidance from the BCS of your future probable self. These impulses will tell you what to do to reach this advanced stage of development. This is the Technique we teach to our phone clients that enables them to do their own research in-between sessions.

Exercise: Reading the Emotional Body

By reading the Emotional Body - another of our theoretical constructs - you may test the Resonance of thoughts, images, emotions, people, places and things, to see what "comes up" for you, as in Issues and Lessons. What you may discover are reasons, rationalizations, barriers that keep you from getting what you want. They possibly resonate with what you DON'T want and so assist in the creation of what you don't want.

As before, simply relax. Achieve your light Trance state. You will be voyaging to the Inner Self with a purpose. The purpose is to discover the specifics of what is holding you back from creating what you want. You will have an assumption, then, that your subconscious does know the specifics about these barriers. As you relax into this state of consciousness, prepare to experience and perceive this data. It may come to you in various ways. Please think in terms of using your counterparts to the outer senses - the Inner Senses - to experience the Emotional Body. You may see it as an image projected onto your "inner eye," so to speak. You may hear, smell and feel something. You will remember this material when you come back to surface awareness. Document what you have learned.

The Practice

The Box

The second part of this exercise entails going over your barriers and putting them in The Box. We spoke of this deceptively simple yet powerful exercise earlier. You have already created your Box and suspended it around your neck. Now figuratively put the negative assessments and barriers, as you understand them, in The Box. As you go about your waking reality, figuratively put all negative material in The Box, material that holds you back from getting what you want. This material could be thoughts, images, emotions, people, places or things, you see. The Box neutralizes the negatives and allows your consciousness to put a positive spin on them.

The next step is to Wonder how these constructs will change so that when you open up The Box to see what has happened, it is filled with positives. This is Wondering in a gentle way, without judgment. It creates a neutral Feeling-Tone. The Wondering allows consciousness to make the appropriate changes to this content to suit you individually according to your Issues and Lessons.

Afterwards, you then Embody these positives. Physicalize them by walking, talking, thinking, imagining them into existence. Please see the chapter on Resonance Dynamics for more information on Wondering. Document what you have learned on the following page.

It may be a good idea to continue your documentation in your notebook or other form after you fill the workpages in this book. This daily exercise is essential, I think, in personalizing and making-your-own the Practice of Intentional Reality Creation.

In The Box

If you feel comfortable doing so, write down on the lines below what you are putting in The Box currently.

_____

_____

_____

_____

Transformed

Again, write down on the lines below what you have put in The Box that is now transformed to a positive, an asset.

_____

_____

_____

_____

Resonance Dynamics

*Resonance is the frequency of creation
in your world...*

Moment of Clarity

These Resonance Dynamics are states of consciousness, and so, potential self-created realities. They are ideas to consider while you are out and about in your waking world. Thus, you find yourself waking up in the moment, as we say, in that, you notice that you are not in the Common Trance. You have a Moment of Clarity in which you say to yourself, "I AM waking up in this moment. I am not asleep now."

You are in your state of Sanctuary, quite probably, for we do suggest you initiate it upon awakening in the morning, and then take it with you into your waking period. This is the baseline, then, this experiencing of Sanctuary with periods of coming out of your Common Trance to notice Moments of Awakening, or clarity. In these moments I suggest you try-out one of the

Resonance Dynamics as a way to extend the momentary awakening into the future.

> **Seth's Soapbox - Moment of Clarity**
> Intermittent moments in your waking reality marked by an increase in existential awareness. Also called the Full Moment, the Moment Point, or Moment of Awakening.

The Five Dynamics

Learning/Finishing-Up

This is an Intentional state of consciousness in which the student is attending to Issues and Lessons during the existence with Loving Understanding and Courage. One has an eye toward approaching the Transition - physical death - with a clean slate. Paradoxically there is positive emotion attached to this state. Death becomes a type of "graduation." After your time of studies, of facing your Issues and learning your Lessons, you retire and consider your past existence. I am speaking literally again here. This is a simplified description of the Soul's journey into the physical.

Remembering/Embodying

In this Dynamic you are Remembering your power as a reality creator. This is the primary Precept of the Ancient Wisdom, "You create your reality." Knowing your power, then, you act, think, and imagine that truth. This Dynamic could also be used with any of the Precepts.

Wondering/Thriving

Here you are Wondering how the Best Case Scenario will unfold in the current moment, and being happily surprised and grateful when it does. Then you attempt to endorse and sustain the BCS on all levels moment-to-moment for as long as possible for the Highest Good for All Concerned.

Awakening/Speaking

In this Moment of Awakening you are aware of your reincarnational existences in multidimensional reality. The other part of this Dynamic entails expressing this greater reality to others through art, teaching, lecturing, writing, and so on. This practice of spreading the message we have called Speaking in my books.

Moment Point/Point of Power

This Dynamic represents the empowerment of the moments of your life. First the Moment Point is acknowledged as your portal to a greater reality. Then you act on that empowering state of consciousness with your Intent to create what your heart desires.

Tools for Awakening

The Lost Perspective

The Resonance Dynamics are your tools for awakening. Because you are an eager student approaching this practice in an amiable, good-humored fashion, it becomes a fun way to spend your day. "How would the Magical Child go throughout life?" you might ask yourself. You are attempting to retrieve this lost perspective through the practices of Resonance Dynamics. Let's look at these Dynamics in more detail…

Learning/Finishing-Up

Learning and Finishing-Up entails this perception of LOOKING for the Lessons in your life, and when they are found, honoring them by admitting responsibility IN THE MOMENT. This would be the full moment of creation, the Moment Point, the potential Point of Power, if you will.

Now the other side of this Dynamic, Finishing-Up, also is experienced in this same Moment Point. When you embrace both aspects of the Dynamic within the Moment Point you create a Point of Power. Within this

Point of Power consciousness assembles the Essential Identity of you-the-reader within physical reality as a Soul who is Learning their Lessons and Finishing-Up. This Essential Identity is then expressed in the Reality Constructs that permeate your Personal Reality Field.

Remembering/Embodying

What occurs within this Dynamic is this... typically, the student is reminded through spiritual literature of some sort, that there are these considerations we call the Ancient Wisdom. Though there are, as I said earlier, instances of this material coming up to consciousness spontaneously, sometimes in quite dramatic ways. Spontaneous healings, spontaneous awakenings, epiphanies and sudden realizations of truth fall into this category. We refer to all of these awakenings, however, as appointments being kept by the participant. The life-changing awakenings are usually planned out ahead of time, as in Past Lives, or in the time before the incarnation in the Home Dimension.

The Remembering process can be initiated and cultivated through some simple practices. In the Trance State you might ask of your Source, your Guidance, "What is the meaning of my life? What are my Lessons?" There is a high probability you will get answers to your questions if you persevere. The answers may come to you in your waking reality. For example: Should you receive the message from your Guides - while you are washing the dishes or taking a walk - that you are here "to serve others with unconditional Love," you might try Embodying this beneficial state of consciousness. The Precept, "You are on Earth to Love one another," may be Embodied by the student with great rewards forthcoming <u>immediately</u>. It is a pleasant state to Embody throughout your waking world.

Wondering/Thriving

Resonance Dynamics is an energy conversation you have with yourself on how to improve realities, to create them more in line with your heart's desire. Your wondering assessments throughout the day interact with your Reality Creation Strategies. What Resonates with the heart's desire is endorsed. What doesn't resonate with the heart's desire is not given creative energy. It is allowed to transform into energies that support the BCS. Please refer to The Box exercise for details on this Technique.

Whenever you check in with yourself on your creative endeavors, you are noticing the difference between what you are creating in the moment, and your heart's desire. In that next moment you Wonder about how your creation will improve. "How much time will it take to create with All That Is _____?" These assessments of Wondering are done playfully, like a child wonders in their imagination.

Now simply asking yourself throughout the day: "What am I creating now?" establishes an emotional Resonance, a context for Intentional manifestation. You are Wondering in a neutral way what is up in your world. It is from the Objective Observer perspective that you make these assessments. There is no ego/intellect involved. The subconscious is engaged also. "I wonder how I will improve this part of my life today?"

What does Thriving mean in this context? Again, that is up to you. Might I suggest, however, that you attach the elements of healing, ecstasy, the Divine, prosperity, and so on, to your demonstrations? You determine how it rolls out in Third-Dimensional Reality, Dear Reader. Your perception <u>creates</u> Reality Constructs that you then behold and appreciate with pleasant surprise, with Loving gratitude, with positive emotion.

Awakening/Speaking

I began this book with a description of the Awakening Ones of your modern era and how they are expressing their visions of the Ancient Wisdom. In this Dynamic you have available a technology of perception that you may use to access and interpret visionary material. You needn't be an "official" artist. The power and authority is in the work itself. This is the awakening phenomenon taken to its logical end, in the creative products of the visionary artist.

Now millions of you are awakening in this timeframe, as you well know. Perhaps you are wondering what to do with this information you are receiving in the Trance State, in the dream state, and in your times of reverie. Art forms and various media, from writing to painting and dance may be used successfully by the Practitioner to spread the message of awakening to others. Indeed, the community of awakening humans is formed in just this way.

A case in point is this work I am doing with Mark and others. The collective of visionary artists and Practitioners of various types is growing exponentially now. Through the Internet and other media the vision is shared with millions of humans from around the world. This is what I mean. This expresses the essence of the Awakening/Speaking Dynamic.

Moment Point/Point of Power

This Dynamic is at the heart of all the others. Throughout my books I have taught how the student of this Teaching may rouse themselves from the slumber of their robotic existence. It happens when you catch yourself "not sleeping." The Moment of Awakening is brief in the beginning. It occurs because you are asking for it to occur, you are asking for magic to occur in your life. The experiencing of a full moment in which you have brief glimpses of your Simultaneous Lives, for example, or waking visions that turn out to be quite accurate predictions, comes as a very pleasant surprise to the novice Practitioner. It is often such a surprise that you miss the opportunity to revel in it, to extend it, to truly enjoy the ecstasy of this state. Be prepared, then, for these moments to present themselves as you practice the Techniques.

We call this perspective The Moment Point. It occurs when you <u>notice</u> that your perception is expanding, even momentarily. You perhaps shake-off the sense of disorientation you may be feeling as you stray from the status quo. Feel your power, then, in that moment of recognition.

This we call the Point of Power. It becomes powerful because you say it is and because you believe it is. If you are a spiritual type, the Point of Power is powerful because you are at that time acknowledging your connection to a power greater than yourself. You may call this energy body God, Goddess, Tree Spirit or Fairy. The power that you Embody during these moments is the power of All That Is to create.

Talking Points

Timing

Different circumstances in waking reality call for a different focus on these Dynamics we are describing. The Visionary, through practice, begins to sense when a different perspective is appropriate. Ideally, it makes sense to continually go about with this appreciation for Positive Reality Creation that is exemplified in the five Resonance Dynamics. You proceed diligently until it becomes second nature. One day you find that you have internalized these Strategies for Intentional creation. At the same time, you might look around you to notice an improved reality.

Rumination Replacement

Now negative ruminations are the creative material for negative realities, as you know. Your Wondering assessments and other Techniques work to replace these negative ruminations with affirmative ruminations. These become the basis for the creation of positive realities. Your consciousness pulls from this material what it needs to create your heart's desire.

You could say that the Practitioner moves from dissonance or resonance with a small "r," that may also be described as static, lower frequencies, the Worst Case

Scenario, unconscious creation... to Resonance, a state that is marked by congruence, higher frequencies, the Best Case Scenario, conscious creation, and so on.

In This Moment

Now the awakening events themselves happen in a split second of perception. Though I ask you to engage in the <u>ongoing</u> assessment and transformation of your Personal Reality using these Strategies, the magic happens, if you will accept this cliché again, in this same moment that you read these words.

Yes, you are asked to engage your Inner Senses in a complete assessment of what you are truly creating in your world. Yet it takes some time, usually, to master these Inner Senses perceptions as well as the multitude of exercises (Humorously) that I proffer to you throughout my new books. Again, the awakening occurs NOW. If you want to save yourself some time and effort, awaken NOW to the truth of your world. I am only being moderately facetious in this statement.

Embodying Precepts

Different than Wondering Assessments, this is practicing the Divine, walking, talking, acting, thinking, feeling, believing in a certain way. Resonance is created here as you juxtapose what you are when you are in your Issues with what you are when you are attempting to Embody your Precepts. Again, the difference, the Feeling-Tone you experience that is the difference between the two states of consciousness is the magical impetus to creating your heart's desire.

> **Seth's Soapbox - Personalizing**
> The true student is distinguished from the dilettante by this dedication to internalizing, physicalizing, and making real the Practice. The student invests all of their energies in these studies.

Personalizing the Dynamics

These Resonance Dynamics yield greater positive effects when the Practitioner personalizes them with their own criteria, just as with the other Essential Metaphors. The process of adapting these potential states of consciousness to your own Journey of Awakening is exactly the same. For example: Suppose you are experimenting with the concept of Learning and Finishing-Up, the first Resonance Dynamic we cover, and perhaps the most important one generally for the student. You are "trying on" this Essential Metaphor to see if you can make some improvements in your life. In other words, whenever you have a full moment of clarity in your waking existence and you remember that you are on a Journey of Awakening, you <u>Embody</u> this Dynamic. So in this momentary awakening you might consider honestly the Lessons of your existence as you understand them.

Remember, your Lessons are easily available to you through asking your friends and family, "What is your opinion of me? What do you think I am here to learn?" Their honest assessments of you are the beginnings of your awakening to the True Self. If you have done self-explorations and you know a bit about your Lessons from that investigation, go with that material. The point is, in this full moment of understanding in your waking world, you are asking yourself this question: "What can I do now in this moment to become more aware of my Lessons, and to, in some way, begin or continue to deal with them for the highest good of all?"

The second component, here, that of Finishing-Up, is a little more complex to negotiate. It entails having an awareness and appreciation for your eventual Transition, your own physical death. Having an ongoing appreciation for your Transition into the non-physical world has great value for you. This state of consciousness holds a quickening of perception, so that you are continually reminding yourself of what is important in your life, and what you must do during your time on the planet. This is not morbid thinking or gallows humor. Paradoxically there is often discovered through this perspective true ecstasy and enjoyment of life. Again, this is not negative thinking but a positive awareness for the truth of your existence.

Attachment

These exercises may appear to be somewhat daunting to the reader. Yes, I am asking you to think about your moment-to-moment reality. I am suggesting that you keep certain principles in mind as you do. It may seem to be a lot of work to some, particularly to those who have been taught that the way to awaken is to NOT focus on the current moment, but to, in a sense, "float" along without attachment. Yet, I believe that my system also allows for a letting-go, a going with the flow in the moment. This occurs simultaneously with the engagement of these other Dynamics, these perspectives. You could almost say that it is in the theorized midpoint of these Dynamics that the release is experienced.

Between Remembering and Embodying, for example, there is an opportunity for release, for experiencing the flow of manifestation. It is in fact this release into the flow of Reality Creation that sustains all of these Dynamics of consciousness manifestation that we have identified. You might call this release, this surrender to the flow, as the experiencing of the Moment Point or the Point of Power that I have described to you in my books. The current moment is all you have, Dear Reader. Surrender into this moment and feel your power.

Holding On and Letting Go

Again, this perspective we espouse is not the experiencing of the free floating moment, the moment of non-attachment. Rather it is a FULL moment of understanding, Courage and transformation. An example: In this full moment I am describing, as you empower it with your Intent, you are engaged in quite the opposite behaviors as are most of your colleagues in physical reality. You are not stumbling forward in the Common Trance, the state of consciousness that supports consumerism and blind obedience to authority. You ARE, in fact, claiming, or perhaps re-claiming the sacred perspective of your ancestors: the Uncommon Trance. This perspective honors the integrity and authority of the individual. Within this state of consciousness you are inner-directed and naturally abide by the suggestions of your greater creative personality. Do you understand this important difference?

Now it is true that I am giving you something more to do than simply fantasize about what breakfast cereal you might buy. Indeed, these practices supplant and spontaneously replace en masse the negative ruminations, self-limiting images and emotional content that tie you to the creation of mundane and negative realities. Choose the appropriate Dynamic according to circumstances.

The Regimens

This accent on the positive has results
in the physical world…

Rituals of Manifestation

The Regimens are in fact Rituals, as we define that term in my new books. They are extended Rituals that the student conducts throughout their waking reality. Now you already know that in this practice we think of the average human in the Common Trance as <u>also</u> conducting a Ritual. The un-awakened human is using their Reality Creation energies in the same ways each moment of each day, day-after-day, to create their mundane reality. This is unconscious creation.

So let us again speak in terms of conscious and unconscious Reality Creation. The un-awakened human Ritually creates subconsciously their mundane realities, just as the awakening human Ritually creates consciously and with Intent their Positive Realities.

The Edge of Creation

Now obviously you can be both: awake and un-awakened. If you are just starting out, it will take some time to master the practices. You will be moving from the realms of the uninitiated into those of the master Practitioner. As you improve your Technique you find that you are continually getting what you want, in a positive sense. Positive Value Fulfillment is what I am describing here.

This is the edge of creation in which you are beginning to see positive effects in your world. It comes after consistent use of the Techniques and Strategies offered in this manuscript. In essence, you are proving to yourself that these systems work. You are the one who must be convinced of the efficacy of this Teaching. How you go about assimilating this material into consciousness and then demonstrating it in physical reality will determine your success and also the timing of your success. Again, I suggest you Courageously and with Loving regard for all, move forward in your existence, manifesting what you Love.

Intentional Creation

Now in their most simplified form, the Regimens entail Embodying the Precepts after you have personalized them, and, if you are the spiritual sort, after you have invoked your Higher Centers Awareness. You might describe the Regimens as a type of "test drive." You are taking your new reality out for a ride to see if you enjoy the effects. If you like what you see, what you are making, continue the Embodiment. Soon it will become a positive habit, replacing the mundane or negative realities you were working on.

> **Seth's Soapbox - Heart's Desire**
> For purposes of this discussion, a Feeling-Tone of Love and a desire for the highest good for all concerned. This construct has power for it is being continuously endorsed with positive energy by the Practitioner.

What is your Heart's Desire?

First it is a good idea to determine what you will be creating. In this simple exercise we will explore which of the realms of human experience you would like to improve with your Ritual practices. Now there are the obvious choices for exploration that include the domains of health, wealth, spiritual understanding, and so on. The Techniques and Strategies that we offer you in this manuscript may be successfully applied to any reality improvement projects you may devise. As we go through the following material, please keep in mind what we have given you thus far. These are simply some general directions on how to go about creating your own Regimens.

Health

Symptoms = Signals

As you address what you feel are probable Issues that you would like to resolve with regards to your health, please think in terms of Signals from the Emotional Body rather than the very loaded term symptoms. Conduct the **Reading the Emotional Body Exercise** from earlier in the book. Ask your Inner Self what might be the true causes of your malady. What you may receive are often literal descriptions of the Issue or perhaps symbolic representations. These readings contain the necessary information for healing and transforming the Issue. Use your own judgment and Inner Senses assessments as you diagnose and treat your malady. Additionally, we have given you hundreds of pages of material on healing in our new books. I refer you there for more specific information.

Depression

The depressed person ritually creates negative value, the fuel for negative, unconsciously-produced realities. In so doing, they incur a muted sense of satisfaction. They have Issues, you see. They are feeling as though they are fulfilling their role as a depressed person by creating the depressed state. But imagine that they are now receiving guidance from an awakening human. They are changing their thoughts, emotions, imagery, and finding that this accent on the positive has results in the physical world. They are producing positive value and it is becoming habitual. Soon they are free from depression. Indeed, soon they are ecstatically co-creating their Personal Reality through their Higher Centers of awareness.

> **Seth's Soapbox - Objective Observer**
> When examining negative realities, such as traumatic events from the past, the Practitioner does not Embody the perspective but looks on dispassionately, objectively, without fear, anger or any emotion whatsoever.

Healing Trauma - The Curse of Memory

Now, many of my readers, because they are human, because they are learning Lessons, they experience emotional injuries. These Learning experiences occur in the younger years, primarily, but obviously one may experience the negative emotions throughout life. The habitual re-creation of negative emotion within consciousness creates these emotional injuries we speak of in the new books. These injuries may be seen within the Emotional Body of the individual, in the dream state, or in other altered states of awareness, such as in Trance, during prayer, during the Guided Visualization, and so on. It is, therefore, to the altered states that we go, as explorers, as Scientists of Consciousness, to discern the specifics of your own emotional injuries.

These events from the past protect themselves. They hide from your view, in a sense, for the content is often so negative, as in shameful, you see, that the ego/intellect cannot handle it. This material is continually forced back into the subconscious, or the underworld, if you prefer, by your conscious mind. Over the years there may be brief attempts by the Soul Self to reveal to the conscious mind these emotional injuries, yet they are most often denied, "repressed," as you say. This continual denial of these secret volatile elements of consciousness serves to give this information more explosive power. This dark side of the human consciousness is thus relegated to the Unknown Reality, where it festers over time.

Now the brief interludes of perception in which this material is accessed by the conscious mind may be appropriately called "flashbacks," using the term from your English vernacular. In a flash, in an instant, the imagery, thought, emotion and other data is served to the present conscious mind for appreciation, for healing, you might say. These breakthroughs into consciousness you might call "the curse of memory," for they do arrive unbidden by the human experiencing them. So in an attempt to redefine these experiences and thus heal them, we may begin to call them the Healing Signals of memory. They are indeed signals from the interior of consciousness as to what MUST be addressed. Let us have an example here to illustrate what we mean.

Childhood Trauma

It is quite common for the human who has been traumatized in childhood to experience these flashbacks in adult life. The volatile material has been repressed successfully over the years, but now the images and other content force themselves upon the waking mind. The Reality Creation is disrupted violently during these events, as the human, usually referred to as "the victim," re-experiences the Feeling-Tone of the traumatic event or events.

It seems to me, that what must change here is the felt sense or Feeling-Tone of the traumatic past that comes to visit. One then revisits the traumatic memories in the Trance State, with an eye toward altering them; altering in memory and thus altering the effects in the flashbacks. One observes the traumatic material as an Objective Observer, without becoming emotionally involved, you see, as though one were watching a movie. Important information is carried out of the Trance State and then documented. Each time the scene is revisited in memory, the Objective Observer notes the particulars with cool detachment. Eventually the flashbacks will be experienced in this Observer Perspective, rather than the traumatized "victim" perspective. It is a case of tuning down the high emotionality and trauma of the event. The cascade of negative emotion will be prevented, as the disturbing material is observed in the cool light of day, you might say. Again, this is simply a change of perspective and so a change of realities.

Path of Healing

Essential Metaphor - You are on a path to your past, to your birth. As you go back in time on this path you see on the side of the road, events, places where you split off parts of your self and left them. The idea is to collect these aspects or parts of self and integrate them into your personality through Intent. You go all the way back to your birth. When you have done this adequately, you can go back beyond and before your birth to the time in between lives, in the Home Dimension and into other lives.

Now if you have issues of abuse from childhood, these issues may be healed from the present. As you walk this path you see different events being recreated on the side of the road. You see where you have left parts of yourself at different stages of development in your life. The idea is to collect these Feeling-Tones and bring them back to the present. This is healing the Soul. It allows you to integrate all of this material and navigate the developmental phase that was interrupted by the trauma.

Change the Past
and the Present Will Take Care of Itself

Now here in this section we will demonstrate how a sense of Good Humor, as in clever punning, may help us initiate a manifestation scenario of positive realities. You already are familiar, I am guessing, with the modern aphorisms regarding the past: "Don't dredge up the past. What's done is done. Look forward." Generally, the past, particularly the past of negative events, traumatic events shall we say, is indeed best forgotten. "Just don't dwell on it," the saying goes, "and it will lose its power over you."

There is some truth to these statements, from my perspective. You do indeed create through a focusing of your energies on the subject matter. And so I do not advise the student who has had a traumatic childhood, for example, to continuously TRY to remember the traumatic events. Without proper preparation, they may make matters worse for themselves. Yet I DO believe that a return to the scenes of the trauma in the imagination, from an Objective Observer's perspective, may be quite healing. Again, this is not done willy-nilly, without regard for the safety of the human. Great preparation is made before the return to master this Observer's Perspective.

Once this is done, the student may safely visit these unfortunate memories, and observe the goings-on objectively, without Embodying these negative memories, in other words. Here is where we use humor to neutralize the negative Feeling-Tone that marks and identifies the traumatic events. ***Change the past and the present will take care of itself.*** It has a sense of the absurd to it yet it is literally true. Over time the Objective Observer creates safety in this retrieval process. The negative emotion loses its sting, its power to wound.

Now having been neutralized, the event may safely be studied, assessed, and TRANSFORMED. The student is quite literally changing their past. When they return to surface awareness from the Trance State they may well experience the cathartic healing of consciousness. In this sense the student recovers, as in going back to retrieve the lost aspects of Soul, rather than recover in the sense of again covering up the negative past. Please note the activity of the double meaning within consciousness.

Physical Health Regimen

Diets

In my past works, I suggested to you that in matters of diet, as in the eating of specific foods, that it was more important what the eater THOUGHT of the food. What matters most are the images, circular thoughts, essential ideas that you-the-eater (Humorously) entertain within your mental environment before, during, and after eating the food. These influences have a very direct effect upon the digestion. So for example, if you eat a small piece of chocolate, say, that is on your FORBIDDEN list of foods, you would have, perhaps, a quite negative reaction to the food. "Chocolate makes me fat," you may say to yourself as you eat it. That statement is a profound suggestion to your subconscious that you immediately, upon eating any chocolate, must begin the process of turning it into fat. Your digestive system will obey dutifully this suggestion as you reinforce it with negative imagery, negative emotion, and so on. In addition, this sets up an unfortunate dis-empowering dynamic in which you play the naughty child that must be punished with obesity by the punitive subconscious.

NOW In This Moment

This reasoning also applies to any attempts at body conditioning through exercise and other physical activities. The important piece here is this: "What do you think of your physical body NOW in this moment?" Now in the moment is when you create your future, you see. Now in the moment is when you must Love yourself, Love your body. If you can see the potential trim and fit physical body beneath the chubby exterior, then you have the right idea. That is your focus, from my perspective. That positive image, that positive Feeling-Tone of Love and success is what may drive your manifestation activities over the course of the Regimen.

Obviously, if what you see before you as you look in the mirror repulses you, you have some important changes to make in your self-assessment activities. That is where you begin, then, to appreciate the body you now have while also anticipating the improvements.

On this Regimen you will be <u>Loving</u> your body into fitness. You Love how you are in this moment, first, and then you move toward the creation of an improved reality moment-to-moment, as you, for example, eat healthy foods, exercise regularly, and all the while you are keeping this Loving Understanding of self intact.

Prosperity Regimen

Prosperity and the Victim Stance

If you feel as though you are experiencing Lack, you have a perspective Issue. You exist within an Abundant Universe, however your Issues act as barriers between you and prosperity. Your beliefs, you see, are actively obscuring your perception of this Abundant Universe.

The Regimens

Let me explain the activity of Resonance at it applies to the Victim. Now Resonance is a dynamic process. It is composed of Light energy fluctuations achieving balance within electromagnetic influences. The Consciousness Units flash on and off, creating different realities in different timeframes. On the basic level, what you focus on consciously, or unconsciously, has a particular vibratory frequency that attempts to replicate itself in physical reality.

On the unconscious level, for example, let us suppose that you have a tendency to create just enough prosperity to sustain yourself, yet never enough to relax and enjoy your life. This is how you view it, your manifestation of your person reality.

This is a type of victim stance, in that, you see yourself as "trying to get ahead," as you say, but it never quite happens.

In my terms, your prosperity evades you for you are creating unconsciously according to less-than-best case scenarios created in your past. These scenarios may have been developed by you in your response to perceived stress, trauma, negative experiences, you see. These are protective strategies that serve to protect you at THAT STAGE of your development: the point in your growth as a Soul in which you sustained the emotional injuries, the damage, you might say, to the Emotional Body. The ego/intellect, the conscious mind attempts to protect you in this way. It keeps from you this negative material. It represses it.

This resonance phenomenon is actively working within your subconscious to match the vibratory frequency of your victim strategy to people, places and things in your physical world. Subconsciously, then, you are creating your reality through this resonance effect, that seeks a match of outside to inside energies.

Holding On And Letting Go

Now there is a time for everything, here, in your Ritual processes. Let me go on a bit about just what I mean with this statement...

Just as this Resonance exhibits both the attractive and repulsive principles, and finds cohesion and momentum "over time," you may find it advantageous to, in a sense, ride this wave of manifestation with your awareness. There is a time for holding on and letting go, resisting/assessing and "going with the flow." You cannot have one without the other in this natural process. It is not "wrong" or "bad" to favor one over the other. It is quite fruitful to embrace both in this practice.

In a very natural way, the student attends to the current moment, for example, with focus and energy. In the next moment, however, you might relax and let go, you see: Distraction. The natural distractions of living will occur for you, taking your focus off of your creative enterprises. Simply let go of your focus in that moment and ride this wave of manifestation. The next moment may call for a return to your focus on the matter at hand. Simply do so, not abandoning the distraction but simply diverting your attention back to the Regimen. This is multitasking. The more you practice, the more proficient you become.

The Bully

Transformation - An example: You are a bully, let us pretend, and you enjoy picking on people, making them miserable. You rationalize your behavior by blaming it on your father, who was also a bully, per the reports from your mother. However, the truth comes out that your father was far from being a bully and was quite Loving and nurturing. He made his Transition at an early time in your life. You were not able to feel fathered completely by this human.

What do you do now? You have an opportunity to change your behavior, to in fact change it to its opposite. You can attempt to Embody the Virtues of Loving Understanding, nurturing, and so on. You will be working on a negative reality you have created for you have found proof that it is based on falsehoods. You have it within you to create these Virtues, as do you all. And so you practice Embodying these opposites of the bully.

Will this practice make an angel out of you, a profoundly Loving and spiritual person? Perhaps. Yet if you do continue this practice of polarizing the Feeling-Tones you have used to create the bully persona, you will undoubtedly improve, in a Soul sense, in the sense of creating progress in your Soul's Evolution.

Your Regimen

Your basic demeanor in these practices, is this: the adult persona presented by the ego/intellect is put to the side, and the child, the magical child, the Wondering child, is allowed to be present.

The Skill-Set

Please gain some proficiency in your Practice before you put together your first Regimen. The Practice is a skill-set that you develop through proving to yourself, in the physical world, that you have the power and knowledge to create. I suggest you do not set yourself up for failure, here. Particularly if this is one of your favorite dysfunctions, to create failure. Please take it slow. Methodical and slow is the best way to go to get your positive results. Then remember, even though the positive feedback from your Ritual is small, perhaps insignificant in comparison to what you see as your BCS, do acknowledge this signal with true gratitude and humility. For it is an indicator that you ARE moving toward your goal. The Universe is responding to your overtures. You are on your way.

My Practice

When I provide ongoing support for clients, I proceed in a particular way. This may help you to create your own program and help you avoid problems.

Now when a client asks me for my insight into a particular Issue that they might have, I remind them that THEY themselves have the solutions. I am only an intermediary here, you see. I am able to observe what the client has in store for themselves as probable trajectories of development, probable realities. Therefore, as you create your Regimens keep this truth in mind, Dear Reader. You already know the answers. You already have created success in your Practice. You are even now quite successful in a probable future from which you may pull inspiration. In other words, please understand this Best Case Scenario that we speak of in this manuscript is real. It is quite apparent to me, and I am certain it will become quite certain to you as you complete your studies.

Secondly, use your Guides as you would a coach or knowledgeable confidante. As we have reminded you before in our second book, the genie of literature and myth is the Energy Personality, the Spirit, the Guide. Knowing this, act as if your Guides have all the answers and it will be so. This can be considered an adjunct Precept to YCYR. Perhaps I would state it thus: "Your Source has all the answers you need to help you manifest your heart's desire." Then, as you Embody this Precept, the Guides will make themselves known to you and make the information available, the information you require, you see, to create your world the way you want it.

Ritual of Sanctuary

Now do personalize the protection Ritual. Put your personality and your personal energy into it. Also it helps to link this creative state of consciousness to a memory, a thought, an image or gesture. In this way you may immediately create a felt sense of protection, security, Love while you are out in your waking world with a mere snap of your fingers. Or perhaps you carry a card in your pocket with the word "Sanctuary" printed on it. Every time you take it out of your pocket and look at it, Sanctuary is created automatically. Again, why does it occur? **It occurs because you create your reality.**

The Regimens

Domains of Living

What areas of your life need improving? What projects are you willing to devote your time and energy to in order to get results? List in order of importance the areas in your life that need this attention. I do think that it is counterproductive to be shy about this, to be fearful that someone may read this material and wonder about your sanity. However, write this in a diary that is secure if you feel that it is necessary.

Now write down what you would like to change.

_____
_____
_____
_____

Current Feeling-Tone

Your first project begins in earnest when you create a Current Feeling-Tone Assessment of the state of the domain of living that you have selected. Do that next.

_____
_____
_____
_____

Best Case Scenario

Now imagine what the BCS would look like when it is finally manifested. Write your BCS on the lines below. Use just a few words to capture the essence, the Feeling-Tone of this construct. I believe that it is important to start this process now. You have the tools to begin. You are ready now to start creating your heart's desire.

_____

_____

_____

_____

The Felt Difference

The Felt Difference is that Feeling-Tone of thought, imagery and emotion that is missing from the BCS. You have assessed your current status quo reality and found some things lacking. You would like to include this material, in other words, in your CURRENT reality. Write down what you have noticed that is missing.

_____

_____

_____

_____

Filling in the Blanks

In this exercise you are taking hold of your Reality Creation in the moment of assessment. You are then including the Felt Difference - the Feeling-Tone of what is missing - in your creative efforts. Using your Intent, allowing your personal power to come forward in that moment, impress this material into your activities, into your perception of your Personal Reality Field.

_____

_____

_____

_____

The Trance State

Further information may be gathered in the Trance State, as we said earlier. You may find it is easier to receive unbiased information in Trance rather than trying to circumvent the agenda of the ego/intellect. Do what works best for you in your Practice.

Also, carry a recording device with you or a simple notebook to document discoveries in the field. Especially note Resonance Factors, those aspects of consciousness that seem to precognate the manifestation. In other words, these glimpses into your future represent your progressed self - the one that enjoys the Best Case Scenario - sending back clues and suggestions from the future. True, this is high-etherics we are suggesting to you in the Practice. However, consider that you are now reading a manuscript dictated by a non-physical being who has been dead for quite some time. I suggest to you that you are ALREADY submerged in the etherics of the Unknown Reality, Dear Reader. You may as well enjoy it. (Humorously)

So you would write down these impulses from the future - the messages from the BCS - and your successes, most assuredly, and also note instances of non-success. Simply note them, however, without berating yourself. This information is crucial to your redirection of energies in your Regimen. Now you know what NOT to do. Now you may do the opposite, in fact. So as you school yourself in this system, be a good teacher, be a kind teacher, be a teacher who models Love for the student.

Probable Outcomes

You are connected to everyone and everything else ...

Feel Your Power

Now the truth is, that you as a Reality Creator may expect an infinite variety of outcomes i.e.; creations. The possibilities are limitless with regards to what you can and do create. In this Practice we speak of these outcomes as a form of feedback of your mentality. What you are thinking about is reflected quite directly back to you from your creations, your Personal Reality. You have thus had a hand in the creation of all that you see in front of you.

Admittedly, you are far more responsible for the creation of your body, shall we say, and your immediate surroundings, than the neighborhood or the city in which you live. Your creative powers are most effective within a 50 foot radius. Feel your power, then, as the creator of realities standing within the magical arena of your Personal Reality Field. Sense it. "Own it," as you say.

Probable Outcomes

Let us cover probable effects of consciousness in the Third Dimension. To begin, as you know, your individual and collective realities are created from limitless probabilities. These probable thoughts, images, emotions, and so on, exist within the etheric, what we also call the pre-manifestation domain. It is from this dimension that your Earthly dimension emerges.

Now all probable effects have a singular charge. This tendency to appear in the particular way of the proposed effect, has, as I said, bioelectric and electromagnetic properties. In your terms, everything that has been or can be conceived by consciousness, exists in the etheric domain. With your imagination, with your consciousness, you consistently add to this repository of potential. By thinking about the goodness of humanity, for example, your positive imagery, emotions, thoughts and other elements seek out their likeness in this pre-manifestation domain, as well as their opposites. The opposites serve to give depth and counterpoint. Through Resonance these correlations are energized, amplified, supported, given life, you see.

In a sense, the negative is inferred through the positive expression, in contrast, you see, in relative contrast. If you wish to think in terms of dynamics within a system, a system of reality, you could theorize that through

Resonance, both the positive and the negative, in addition to all expressions in between these two polarities, are expressed to the nth degree throughout the past, present, and future. Value Fulfillment occurs simultaneously with this expression.

Updated Projections

Thus the evolving experience of the awakening student represents these continually updated projections of the Essential Identity into the Third Dimension. This is your life. As a human on this trajectory of Soul Evolution, your awakening consciousness is reflected in the ongoing products of your consciousness: your body, your environment, your life.

Dear Reader, you are always in-tune with your creations, your Personal Reality. You are always getting what you ask for. "But Seth," you may say, "I am certainly not getting what I want. I am poor, sickly and quite unhappy. How can you say that?" In my presentations to you in physical reality we rely on a basic assumption that you are the creator of your world. As I said, you create your reality, your Personal Reality Field. You are connected to everyone and everything else in the created Universe through the CUs. Thus, as an individual you create your Personal Reality and as a collective of humans, you create your consensus realities. On the basic level, then, you look out in front of you and see your part of this Universe: your home, your friends and family, your job site, and so on. Now on the collective, progressed level of perception, the Visionary State, you might call it, when you look out in front of you, you may be witnessing your multidimensional reality. Visions of other lives may play out before you or upon the inner screen of your creative imagination. So let us here differentiate between these two states of consciousness perception and thus Reality Creation.

Resonance Factors

You create your reality. Each moment you create your part of the manifestation and allow others to participate. As a collective of manifesters - and this includes the elements and other non-living constructs - you create within your Personal Reality Field this ongoing drama: the world. Because you do this unconsciously, for the most part, it does entail an investigation to get to the bottom of these processes. For example: Consider that you-the-reader are perhaps engaged in a creative project of the type we are describing. You are focusing on something, attempting to manifest an improved reality for yourself or others, or perhaps you are attempting to Resonate into existence a useful object, such as a new car, appliance, or some such thing.

Regaining Focus

Now you get what you focus on, whether it is subconscious or conscious focusing. So assume that you ARE remembering in this moment that you are magically engaged in creating what you want. You are focused consciously on the goal. You are perhaps visualizing the object or state of consciousness in detail, here, moment-to-moment. But what if you are losing this focus as you become engaged in taking care of a mundane matter that seeks attention? What often occurs at these times is an appearance by one of these stimulants, one of the Resonance Factors, that encapsulates, in a sense, the creative project for you up to the point of departure, so that you can remember where you left off when you return after the distraction with no loss of momentum.

Again, it is a Feeling-Tone. It has imagery, it has emotion, it has circular thought attached to it. Then, you might take care of the distraction and afterward return to your project of manifestation. You might do this by remembering the Feeling-Tone, the summation from the BCS, the Resonance Factors that engaged you directly before you broke your state. Embody those Factors and begin again on your creative project. This is a simple way to keep your manifestation projects on track, in spite of the inevitable distractions in physical reality.

The Unhappy Human

Let's end this chapter with another quiz…

What would you expect to be the probable outcomes of the Reality Creation projects of an unhappy, spiteful, angry human? Can you name some specifically? I would suggest a few that come to mind. Let me speak about them if I may:

This human would probably experience unhappy, unfulfilling outcomes. Because they were creating through the emotional templates of anger, spite, unhappiness, they would experience probable outcomes that veritably <u>ring</u> with these negative states of consciousness. They would be choosing, probably unconsciously, from this pool of negative emotion, the particulars of emotional nuance with which they would color their Reality Creation efforts.

As this person awakens from sleep, then, perhaps it is automatic for them. They have experienced days, weeks, months and perhaps YEARS of unhappy, spiteful, and angry states of consciousness. They have become an expert at creating these states, simply because they have been at it now for quite some time. So rather than bounding out of bed, eager to approach the day, perhaps they are pulling the covers over their head, to attempt to keep the day at bay. Then, as they are forced to react to the alarm that they have programmed into their alarm clock, they begrudgingly roll out of bed and trudge into the bathroom.

Scowling

There this unhappy person perhaps scowls at their less-than-attractive form in the mirror. Defects of appearance are noted and perhaps amplified to muse over later. As this person attempts to begin their day, they are already drawing negative correlations between the things they see in their environment and what they are experiencing inside, in the consciousness, in the personal identity. They will then spend the rest of they day validating their negative state of consciousness by noting other negative correlations that they discover in the home, on the job, everywhere they go. Thus you could say that the ego notes the perceived negative characteristics within the Personal Reality as the intellect proves them to be quite true; <u>a fact of life</u>, as it were. This is how beliefs are formed.

~~~~~~~

Outcomes

Please begin to note on the lines below, the perceived outcomes of your Practice and Regimens.

Q and A with Seth

Seth, opposites attract say the laws of physics, yet you maintain that Resonance is also based on a similarity of vibration.

Let me clarify this for you. You know that everything that can exist is created NOW, in the eternal moment that holds all. Yet you exist within the confines of a linear time construct that depends on these laws of cause and effect, and others. If it helps you, please think of this Resonance as a process THAT INCLUDES what you call the attractive principle, the principle stated in your so-called Law of Attraction. It exists within the activity of the CUs. The CUs are active multi-dimensionally, past, present, and future, in your terms. They express themselves as different Reality Constructs in different dimensions of time. As these units of energy come together through an affinity of shared attributes, THE OPPOSITES ARE ALSO PULLED TOGETHER, expressing what you might call the "glue" of consciousness: that which gives thought form. This occurs in somewhat the opposite manner as when centrifugal forces separate out the constituents of a liquid substance with matter dissolved within it. Bioelectric forces, meaning, the energies that animate ALL substances, in league with natural cosmic magnetic forces, all at the same time, remember, in this spontaneous process, in a sense, "push and pull" the CUs into the desired form of consciousness manifestation: consciousness in action, evolutionary consciousness expressing itself in all ways, in all forms, at all times. There is a Holographic Insert attached to this message, if you would care to look for it in your mental environment. Please note my use of the word *desired* as a pun. (Humorously)

Would you comment on your statement that the visionary leader is becoming known in all collectives. This is a question from an Internet reader?

Yes, it is cyclical. The Changing of the Guard is underway. The Shift in Consciousness transforms all. Specifically, for the interested citizen, those of you who are waking up, it is this Resonance in action, once again. Now the cycle of domination is changing. The idea that you must conquer the Earth, that to succeed you must dominate others, that the proper way to raise a child is to punish them when they misbehave, these concepts are giving way during this cycle of change. A cycle, a natural cycle of manifestation, implies that changes occur quite naturally, in the natural order of things, you might say. This is the case with The Shift. The dominators have had their say for many generations on Earth. They have created a crisis situation worldwide with their selfish behaviors. In the natural order of things, do you see how this Shift brings up the Ancient Wisdom that contains NEW ideas, NEW images, NEW and positive means of creating, behaving, Loving in the world?

I hope that you sense my irony, once again, as we speak in terms of the NEW ideas that the Ancient Wisdom brings. They ARE new to many of you, for you have practiced over these many years, the way of forcing yourselves on others and on your environment. It is, from my perspective, completely and utterly expected that the "season" of the dominators would give way, in time, to the era of the Lovers of Earth, of humanity.

Anything on Resonance and awakening?

Yes Mark. Your changing roles as an awakening human reflect this learning of Lessons through FACING your Issues. Let me explain. Now you begin where you are.

Resonance - Manifesting Your Heart's Desire

You are not yet awakened but you are getting there. You have discovered that you have Issues, spiritual Issues that are DEMANDING your attention. There is no room for denial. There is no time left for intellectualizing away these basic Issues. You are compelled to take to heart, for example, the admonishments of your friends, family, and colleagues. This advice may range from the negative through the positive, as in, "You are a walking ego. You harm others through your insensitivity," to "You should really get out more. You could find a great partner if you were to make the gesture, go out, meet people." As you act on the advice of others, or perhaps on promptings from other sources, such as the nonphysical beings, you are expanding your boundaries, your beliefs, your societal role.

In this case, your collective consciousness is Resonating with the ancient civilizations. In those prototypical cultures the highest good for all concerned was practiced in all endeavors. These important life-sustaining, healing messages enter your awareness as impulses, impulses, perhaps, to do good, give to others, to work on yourself and become a better human being. As your personal consciousness Resonates with these messages, you add to the collective Resonance, simply because you are connected to the collective through your thoughts, through your images, and so on. Thus, you achieve your particular state of Resonance with the Ancient Wisdom even as you contribute to the collective state of Resonance by your CHANGING of behaviors, emotions, imagery. "Waking up," you call it. You are waking up to your responsibilities to create for the highest good.

As you claim this responsibility as your own, your "personal credo," so to speak, you quite naturally, again, assume a leadership position within your family, your town, your state, country and world. You are modeling for others this assuming of the awakened experience. You then Resonate with other visionary leaders. You come together to make plans for the future. You work as a collective for the betterment of your collectives, large and small. Does that answer your question?

Yes, quite inspirational. Thanks Seth.

Seth, what is the relationship between Lessons and your theory of Resonance?

A quite basic relationship. Now remember that these are metaphors for the projection of All That Is into your system. Lessons is our Essential Metaphor for why the human comes to the physical plane. We suggest it is to experience these Lessons of Value Fulfillment, as the Virtues of Humanity are endorsed and Embodied, or perhaps denied and vilified. However, the Lesson is a Lesson BECAUSE you are noticing it and interpreting it as a Lesson. You create your own reality, and as you do YOU are the value-fulfiller, whether it is the fulfillment through behavior, emotion, imagery and thought of physical violence, as in a perpetrator of violence upon others, or as is the case with a do-gooder type, who bestows goodness, Love, compassion on others. In both cases values are fulfilled. In both cases Lessons are learned.

Now let us look at the two examples in terms of frequency of vibration. We have suggested that negative emotion holds a lower vibration than does positive emotion. This is our premise upon which we build our theory of Resonance. In one example, the subject builds negative Reality Creations with negative emotions. This low frequency resonates with negative emotion everywhere. Within the collective gestalt of emotion, within the Collective Unconscious, your negative emotions resonate with other similarly-created negative emotions of humanity. You could say that this amalgam of negative emotion that is seeking out other "like" emotions within the consciousness field, eventually, through resonance, finds a home for itself. These "homes" we call the Gestalts of Consciousness, the foundational elements of Reality Constructs of all types, including of course, Reality Constructs of air, of ideas, of soil and stone, and so on. But again, these theorized activities of consciousness are simply metaphors for the exceedingly complex activities of the Consciousness Units.

Seth, you said you wanted to comment on the topic, "Those Who Follow Shall Lead."

Now as you refuse advice from authority figures, you quite naturally learn how to trust YOURSELF. Again, this is a learned habit, like anything else in your reality. What you focus on habitually, whether subconsciously or consciously, you tend to create. The Courageous step of relying on your Inner Self to provide the information you seek, becomes a faithful expectation that you will receive what you desire and need. Over time it does indeed become second nature. You might also call it a faithful, trust-filled precognition that what you ask for is being provided.

This is the Ancient Wisdom, in fact, and this communication stream arrives from your greater Gestalt of Consciousness. It is personalized, this stream of data, for your perception. It is tuned to your frequency, specifically, to the frequency of your awakening Spirit. Thus, the awakening human becomes an expert on their own unfolding consciousness. And simply because you are connected to everyone/thing in the Universe, you are also mastering a perception of the macrocosm here: the greater gestalt you may call All That Is.

Seth, how does what you just transmitted relate to Resonance? Can you simplify this for the reader?

Yes, let me relate this to my concept of the Visionary Leader. First, you are awakening now. I believe I may safely say that at this time. You are reading this material because you are interested in the Unknown Reality and other metaphysical concepts. You are of this type, quite probably, that honors the sacred within consciousness. You look for it, you find it sometimes, and allow it to transform you, to wake you up. As this occurs within the consciousness of, let us say, a production worker in an automobile plant, you may feel prompted to tell others about your experiences. As you share your findings with others you catalyze the awakening experience in them. Each of you in this collective of awakening humans becomes YOUR OWN leader. You are leading yourself away from authority and to your own truth.

Q and A with Seth

This is the Visionary Leader: the one who learns how to access their truth, teaches it to others, and then leads by example, you see. The Virtues of Humanity are their leadership principles. The highest good for all concerned is their focus of creation, of manifestation. The awakening human, in short, Resonates their improved reality into existence, by allowing these inner Precepts we call the Ancient Wisdom to replicate themselves in the Third Dimension. The etheric is physicalized through this process of Resonance. The sacred is established in the physical world for the greater improvement of all that exists in your world.

Now, your primary Lesson in this reality concerns how you, as an individual with your own aspects of personality, will respond to negativity. You are on Earth to experience negativity and your reactions will determine how long you will stay in the physical body in any particular incarnation, as well as other particulars of physical existence, such as when and if you shall return to a human form to experience the opportunity to deal with your Issues and Lessons: those experiences you have avoided or not dealt with properly.

I do not wish to compare this phenomenon with the stories from your world scriptures. For the most part, these stories quite literally HIDE FROM VIEW the essential meaning of the reincarnational journey. That is quite simply because these manuscripts were written by human beings with an agenda, an agenda of the ego. What we are here discussing is the Soul's agenda. The Soul sends out particles of itself, of its energy, into human babies to grow with the human and experience the Lessons.

Beyond your initial Lessons of reacting appropriately to negativity come the Lessons particular to individuals. Your focus, your perspective, your orientation, the lenses of belief through which you create your reality, determine to the most minute detail the presentation of your Personal Reality Field before you. It is feedback, it is a recapitulation, it IS a replication of the interior processes of consciousness. The reality constructs of your world assemble into solidity at the bequest of ALL consciousnesses involved.

Seth, what's the connection between Resonance and synchronicity?

Before I attempt to answer your question, first allow me to set the stage here a bit. Now remember, you *are* a Reality Creator. You *are* a manifester. So you *are* already, as we speak, resonating your Personal Reality Field into being, into existence, you see. The problem may be that you are manifesting <u>un</u>consciously. As you do, you create reality <u>through</u> the templates of your Issues. These are your beliefs about yourself and your world. This expression of your unconscious in the physical world may not be to your liking, therefore. You may in fact find yourself always making the same mistakes, and so, always creating less-than-satisfactory realities.

These are synchronicities also, the negative events, the negative realities. They are showing you that you <u>are</u> on a path of development and that you <u>must</u> change your ways. The negative reality creator looks around them and says to themselves, perhaps: "Why do I always create the same failed relationships?" "Coincidentally," this person has, once again, established a relationship with a new person, within a different environment, also, possibly, in a different context entirely, that eventually becomes the "failed" relationship they feared. Might I suggest that the resonance in this case, the Feeling-Tone created here that resonates within consciousness, is of a negative nature? You may also refer to it as a series of ongoing harbingers of negative events; omens warning you of future negativity. But you are creating unconsciously and so you are not consciously aware. Your conscious perceptions overlook this data, they deny this information, they intellectualize and "explain away" these harbingers.

Resonance - Manifesting Your Heart's Desire

Your consciousness is unconsciously, automatically resonating your failed relationship into existence, just as it always does, just as it always will, unless you wake up to what you are up to.

Now additionally, because we are being precise and brief in our new book… synchronicity is a perception, and thus, a state of consciousness in which connections are made by the observer. The mundane definition might suggest these are coincidental connections, perfectly un-extraordinary perceptions of the brain as it attempts to "make sense" of seemingly similar sensory input. This is true to a degree. However, let us provide our own definition with my theory of Reality Creation in mind. Synchronistic sensings are signals from the Soul-self to the ego/intellect. They are meant to draw you into the moment. They are the basis of awakenings, the momentary awakenings we speak of in the new material. I often suggest to you, Mark, that these coincidental experiences are telling you that you <u>are</u> on a path of awakening, even though you may not admit it. Indeed, if you were to observe and honor the synchronistic connections being made within your consciousness, you may possibly discover that <u>everything</u> is connected. The deeper you go, the more that is revealed. Over time, when you have learned how to "ride" these synchronous moments into the "future," you find that you <u>are</u> awakening to your greater creaturehood. The sensings of your Simultaneous Lives, the workings of the Universe, the secrets of Reality Creation become your habitual, ongoing experience.

Ray G. says: I have one that might be beneficial to a large portion of your readers. Last year I spent about 15 or 20 minutes a day almost everyday in a semi-meditative state visualizing a desired outcome for around five months. My question is: "When is long enough, long enough?" "How or when do I start expecting to see evidence and how does one get into the 'law of attracting' mindset without feeling guilty about being materialistic?" "What is a good practice for changing those beliefs?" To summarize:

#1.   How many minutes per session?
#2.   What length of time?
#3.   How does one create a feeling of expectation?
#4.   How to change beliefs?
#5.   Do I visualize myself as if I were looking thru my eyes counting a handful of money or do I visualize it as if I were

watching a movie of myself counting a handful of money?

Let me answer these pertinent questions to the best of my ability. (Humorously)

Now first, the amount of time you spend in your meditations is up to you. We suggest at least 15 minutes per day, as early in the day as possible. This sets you up for an active day of conscious manifesting. And remember, your Sanctuary is "intact" at ALL times during your waking period. You may even bring it into the dreamstate by ritually focusing on it prior to sleep.

Number 3, the key here, for you and others, I believe, is to bring this Sanctuary with you out into the world and <u>bring</u> this meditative state and its contents and energies into the world with you. This is your expectation, you see. This is your attempt to continuously, or at least intermittently (Humorously) Intentionally create your Personal Reality.

The expectation is felt in the demonstration, your faithful anticipation - in the small moments of awakening from the Common Trance - of the manifestation you are considering. Not to repeat myself too much here, but you seek to <u>Embody</u> the Feeling-Tone of your anticipated creation. If you read my books you will get this message as well as the subtext, if you are open to it. I have provided numerous Strategies for belief change in this and other books. The simplest is to identify the limiting belief - identify its Feeling-Tone - and then Embody, once again, its opposite, or its improved condition with <u>gusto</u>! You are not merely begging for a miracle, here. You are the Reality Creator in league with All That Is.

Your Question 5 is excellent. My answer is this: If you are examining painful material from the past - childhood abuse, let us say - assume the Observer's Perspective and disentangle yourself from the drama you are witnessing. If you are in the Trance State and you are meditating on the Abundant Universe, yes, you <u>would</u> Embody that image, emotion, thought as completely as you could, within the safety of your Sanctuary.

In conclusion, if you are feeling guilty about being materialistic and you are experiencing Lack, I would suspect religious conditioning is at fault. As you know from the current manuscript, you are already living in an Abundant Universe. Perhaps your unnecessary feelings of guilt act like walls around you that prohibit your perception of this Universe. You might attempt to practice our Consecutive Positive Assessments exercise in which the student focuses on finding something positive in each moment. That becomes the focus over time until you <u>are</u> seeing, for yourself, this prosperous lifetime, for you are creating it.

Again, 15 minutes per day is a good start, but the magic happens when you bring all of your waking faculties to bear on this project. Each moment of your day, then, becomes an opportunity for experiencing the transcendent moment, the moment of awakening to the Abundant Universe.

Epilogue

It has been a pleasure to cast a light for these brief moments onto the Unknown Reality. This Ancient Wisdom is now yours to keep. Once the door has been opened to this kingdom, as in the reading of a book on the subject, such as the one you are reading in this moment, it cannot be closed. Indeed, we look upon these decisions of readers to actually read our books and do the exercises as keeping appointments. You are keeping an appointment with the Seth entity and with yourself also, as you go about internalizing this material. As I have said before, that is why it sounds so familiar to you, that is why it sounds so true. You are always doing this. You are always, in all of your lives, seeking out this Ancient Wisdom material and then being happily surprised and also mystified as to how it came about this time.

I salute you now as a faithful follower of the Light. Until we meet again...

Ritual of Sanctuary

The Ritual of Sanctuary was presented to readers in our book on ***Soul Evolution*** when we first began to emphasize direct exploration of the Unknown Reality. We felt that the reader would require some personalized protection in their experimentation.

The most simple form of the Ritual is to imagine, prior to psychic pursuits, a golden Light surrounding you. Nothing harmful can penetrate this field of Light. It has a healing protective influence. You may certainly use this simplified form while you go about creating your own Ritual.

The object here is to generate positive energies with your creative consciousness. Try listing on a piece of paper your positive beliefs and ideas that denote security, peace, and protection. The next step would be to, perhaps artistically, distill these potent concepts down into an image, statement, or physical object that Resonates with the protective energies. Naturally you may include gestures, visualizations, or any other evocative materials. Practice your Ritual until you can create at-will the state of Sanctuary within your own consciousness. Only you will know when you are successful.

Glossary

Definitions for the concepts Seth discusses in this book.

All That Is - The energy source from which all life sprung throughout the multitude of Universes, transcending all dimensions of consciousness and being part of all. Also referred to as the Logos and Evolutionary Consciousness.

Ancient Wisdom - The knowledge of the magicians, shamans, witches and healers of the past.

Awakening - As the Ancient Wisdom is remembered by humanity, an awareness of the greater reality is experienced by individuals.

Beliefs - Ideas, images, and emotions within your mental environment that act as filters and norms in the creation of Personal Realities.

Bleedthroughs - Momentary experiencing of lives being lived in other tirmeframes and other systems of reality.

Co-creation - You co-create your reality with the limitless creative energies of All That Is.

Consciousness Units (CUs) - The theorized building blocks of realities. Elements of awarized energy that are telepathic and holographic.

Courage - Courage and Loving Understanding replace fear and anger in the creation of Positive Realities.

Denial - The ego/intellect prevents the learning of Lessons by denying the truth of the matter.

Dimensions - Points of reference from one reality to the other with different vibrational wavelengths of consciousness.

Divine Day - The student attempts to live a complete waking day while maintaining contact with the Energy Personality.

Divine Will - The will is potentiated through ongoing contact and communication with Beings of Light. Also called Intent.

Ego/Intellect - The aspect of the personality that attempts to maintain the status quo reality.

Ecstasy - The positive emotion experienced in contact with the Divine.

Embodiment - Precepts are lived in the creation of improved realities.

Energy Personality - A being capable of transferring their thought energy inter-dimensionally to physical beings and sometimes using the physical abilities of those beings for communication.

Entity - Being not presently manifested on the physical plane. Also known as a Spirit.

Essential Identity - A truthful representation of the personality as perceived with the Inner Senses.

Feeling-Tone - Thoughts, images, sounds and assorted sensory data that represent a particular state of consciousness, event, or existence.

Glossary

Fourth-Dimensional Shift - Consciousness expands as the individual experiences an awareness of all Simultaneous Existences. Also called Unity of Consciousness Awareness.

Gestalts of Consciousness - Assemblages of Consciousness Units into Reality Constructs of all types.

gods - Consciousness personalized and projected outward into reality. A self-created projection of the developing ego.

Holographic Insert - Teaching aid of the non-physical beings. Multisensory construct experienced with the Inner Senses.

Incarnation - To move oneself into another life experience on the physical plane.

Inner Sense - The Soul's perspective. Both the creator and the perceiver of Personal Realities.

Intellectualization - The aspect of the psyche that attempts to figure things out so that the status quo is maintained.

Intention - See Divine Will.

Lessons - Chosen life experiences of the Soul for further spiritual evolution.

Light Body - The etheric body of refined light.

Love - Love with a capital L is the force behind manifestation in the Third Dimension.

Moment Point - The current empowered moment of awakening. Exists as a portal to all points past, present and future and all Simultaneous Lives.

Mystery Civilizations - Foundational civilizations largely unknown to modern science. Some examples are Atlantis, Lemuria and GA.

Negative Emotion - Habitual creation of negative emotions creates enduring negative realities.

Negative Entities - Negative energies that roam the Universes in pursuit of their own power to dominate.

Percept - Perception creates reality in the Third Dimension through the Inner Senses.

Personal Reality Field - The radius within your self created world within which you have the most control in the creation of Reality Constructs.

Precept - Empowered concepts of manifestation. Example: you create your own reality.

Reality - That which one assumes to be true based on one's thoughts and experiences. Also called Perceived Reality.

Reality Creation - Consciousness creates reality.

Reincarnational Drama - Soul Family drama enacted to teach the participants a Lesson in Value Fulfillment.

Scientist of Consciousness - The researcher studies the phenomena within the Personal Reality Field by testing hypotheses in experimentation. See Precept.

Glossary

Observer Perspective - Self-created aspect of consciousness that sees beyond the limitations of the ego/intellect. An intermediary position between the ego and the Soul Self.

Seth - An energy personality essence that has appeared within the mental environments of humans throughout the millennia to educate and inspire.

Simultaneous Lives - The multidimensional simultaneous experiences of Souls in incarnation.

Soul - The non-physical counterpart to the physical human body, personality, and mentality. The spiritual aspect of the human.

Soul Evolution - The conscious learning of Lessons without denial or intellectualization.

Soul Family - The group of humans you incarnate with lifetime after lifetime to learn your Lessons together.

Spiritual Hierarchy - Beings of Light who have mastered multidimensional levels of experience throughout the Universes and have moved on to higher service in the evolution of all Souls.

The Christ - The embodiment of The Christ in your World. Also called World Teacher. First described in Seth Speaks.

The Council - Members of the Spiritual Hierarchy. Highly evolved beings that advise Souls on incarnations for their spiritual evolution.

The New World - The Positive Manifestation.
The Vanguard - Advocates for humanity and Mother Earth who incarnate together to lead progressive movements of various kinds.
Third Dimension - The physical plane of Earthly existence.
Trance State - The relaxed, focused state of awareness that allows the Scientist of Consciousness to conduct experiments and collect data.
Value Fulfillment - Consciousness seeks manifestation of itself into all realities via the fulfillment of all values.
Visionary - Reincarnated magicians, shamans, witches and healers in this current timeframe.

*I think we're going to have to do a book or two or three
or four or many more to get the masses
to see the problem* ... Seth

MORE BOOKS?

Seth has promised to continue to communicate with us to further the awakening of humanity. This means that there will be an ongoing source of current, inspirational messages available from: **Seth Returns Publishing**

Communications from Seth on the Awakening of Humanity
9/11: The Unknown Reality of the World
The first original Seth book in two decades
The Next Chapter in the Evolution of the Soul
The Scientist of Consciousness Workbook
Thought Reality
The Healing Regimen and Spiritual Prosperity

The Trilogy
All That Is - Seth Comments on the Creative Source
Mystery Civilizations - Seth Answers Reader's Questions on Legendary Civilizations
Soul Mate/Soul Family - Contains the Soul Mate Project

Seth - A Multidimensional Autobiography
Resonance - Manifesting Your Heart's Desire

To order visit **sethreturns.com** or **amazon.com** Or ask your local bookstore to carry the new Seth books.

www.ingramcontent.com/pod-product-compliance
Lightning Source LLC
Chambersburg PA
CBHW022305060426
42446CB00007BA/602